An American Deception's

Revealing America's Dark Skinned Past

Vol. 1

Red SilverFox Thunderbird

REVEALING AMERICA'S DARK SKINNED PAST VOL. 1
Copyright © 2018 by Red SilverFox Thunderbird.

All rights reserved. Printed in the United States of America. No part of this book may be used or reproduced in any manner whatsoever without written permission except in the case of brief quotations embodied in critical articles or reviews.

For information contact :
InDEED- Indigenous Education Enrichment and Development
http://indedu.org/reneebio/

Book and Cover design by LN Gibson
ISBN: 978-0-9857375-5-9

Second Edition: March 2018

REVEALING AMERICA'S DARK SKINNED PAST

Table of Contents

INTRODUCTION 5

CLOVIS PEOPLE WERE NOT THE FIRST PEOPLE 9

THE MOUND BUILDERS 15

TYPES OF MOUNDS 19

MOUND SITES 1

THE OLMEC CIVILIZATION 11

THE DESTRUCTION OF ANCIENT CITIES AND ARTIFACTS 25

"TO THE WAYS OF THE WHITE PEOPLE" 33

EPILOGUE 42

ABOUT THE AUTHOR 46

BIBLIOGRAPHY 49

REVEALING AMERICA'S DARK SKINNED PAST

INTRODUCTION

BROWN SKINNED PEOPLE, from very light to dark, dark brown have existed in the Americas for many thousands of years. However, history wants us to believe that the existence of Black people in the western hemisphere began with the African slave trade.

It is from this falsehood that many people in the United States have been manipulated into thinking that all slaves came from Africa and the Black populations in the United States are the descendants of those Africans. While many blacks may have some African genetics in their bloodline, that should not be the determining factor to define all Blacks in the United States as African American. Many blacks have European genetics in their bloodline, but they are not defined as European Americans!

REVEALING AMERICA'S DARK SKINNED PAST

Many African Americans have been told by their ancestors that they have 'Indian blood'; however, over time, this information has been dismissed by most (even though this oral history continues to get passed down through the generations). Traditionally, Africans and Native Americans passed history down orally through tribal elders (Native) or the tribal griot (African). That the Indians like the Africans in America relied upon oral media for the transmission of their history from one memorial generation to the next, meant that the dissolution of their social structure would destroy their history and therefore complete the erasure of their existence.[1]

That dissolution or disbanding of the social structure, or in other words, terminating the glue which held those societies together, was the key that was needed to destroy the passing down of family history, and consequently destroy the moral being of the people. When a people are broken morally, it is easy at that point, to mold and shape their minds to be what you want them to be, and to erase the things you want them to forget.

The annihilation of the family structures practiced on the brown skinned people in what became the United States, namely the Indigenous Americans and the Africans, became a more imperative operation within the Indigenous communities. The conquering and colonizing Europeans needed to remove everything that would not benefit their existence in the newly occupied territories; and the one thing that stood the most in their way was the Indigenous Americans. While many indigenous cultures were decimated through disease, warfare and slavery, what wasn't put into the equation was the resiliency of the dark skinned people that the Europeans encountered upon their arrival here in the Americas.

The true history of the indigenous people of the United States, and in particular the entire eastern and southeastern United States, has been banished into non-existence, and the true identities of those people have not been taught. The fact is if the real history and identities of the indigenous people of America were revealed, we would know that the homeland of millions of Black Americans is actually here in the United States, and not in Africa as currently explained.

It is time for everyone to comprehend that history was/is not totally honest in its interpretation of the facts of the indigenous people of the Americas, and that many Blacks in the United States are the descendants of those Indigenous Americans.

REVEALING AMERICA'S DARK SKINNED PAST

Clovis People Were Not the First People

HOW THE AMERICAS GOT POPULATED remains in much speculation. The theory which has a stronghold in history books is the migration theory that humans migrated out of Europe, into Asia, over the Bering Strait, and down and across into the Americas. This migration would have taken place between 12,000-15,000 years ago after the last ice age melted the ice on the Bering Strait to expose the land for the humans to cross. This theory was developed in the 1700's and has basically remained unchanged.

While I am sure that many humans entered the

REVEALING AMERICA'S DARK SKINNED PAST

Americas across the Bering Strait, this could not have been the only way humans entered the Americas. The problem with the Bering Strait theory is that there is much archeological evidence that humans existed in the Americas before the Ice Age ended.

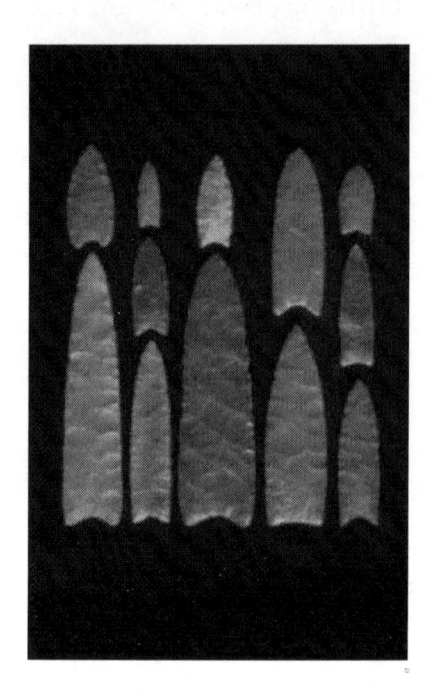

Clovis people, who are considered to be the first humans in the Americas, are said to have entered the Americas across the Bering Strait from Asia. However, current archeological and biological evidence does not support the assumptions of the Clovis migration theory about Paleo and Indian migration routes...[Scientists] studied skulls, genetic patterns and dental variations to verify the first entry of Mongolians [Asians] into the Americas that only began after 3,000 B.C....[2] The Clovis points that were found 9,400 years ago [in the U.S.] do not match the points found in Asia, the land where they were said to originate.[3] It would appear that the Clovis technology was not an Asian import; it was invented here [in the U.S.].[4]

So if these points were not Clovis, where did they come from? It appears that "there is a growing body of archeological evidence suggesting that there were other people here...It appears that the Clovis people were not the first people...".[5] So if Clovis are not the first people here, who were?

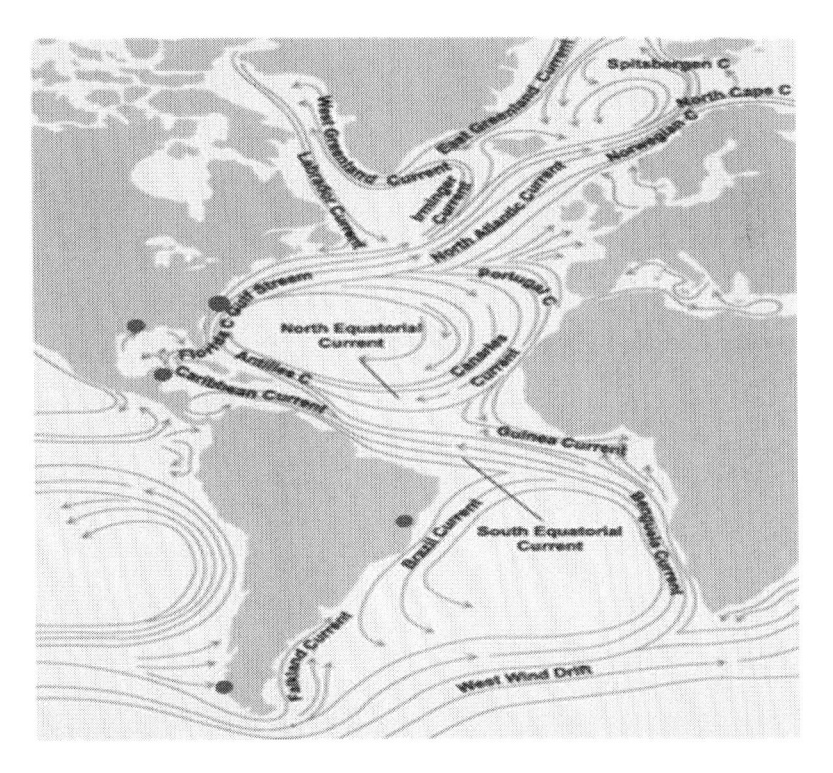

REVEALING AMERICA'S DARK SKINNED PAST

There are increasing indications that there were early migrations into the Americas that pre-date the thawing of the ice glaciers which covered all of Canada and half of the United States. Sites in Chile, Brazil, Mexico, Oklahoma and South Carolina "suggest that humans were in the Western Hemisphere as early as 30,000 years ago to perhaps 60,000 years ago."[6] These sites are all along the Atlantic Ocean currents, except for Chile (which is only 400 miles away from the Atlantic Ocean), which would suggest a migration of humans straight out of Africa to the Americas. Clues from the skeleton's skulls hint that the people may not be of northern Asian descent, which would contradict the dominant theory of New World settlement.

Ivan Van Sertima who was an associate professor of African Studies at Rutgers University describes the Atlantic currents in his book 'They Came Before Columbus' as "...currents that move with great power and swiftness from Africa to America. These currents may be likened to marine conveyor belts. Once you enter them you are transported (even against your will, even with no navigational skill) from one bank of the ocean to the other."

Recent evidence found deep (over four meters) in the soil in Allendale County, South Carolina has uncovered, through radiocarbon dating, sediments "with two dates of 50,300 and 51,700 on burnt plant remains."[8] Dr. Albert Goodyear, archeologist for the University of South Carolina said, "This is the oldest radiocarbon-dated site of human activity in North America..., [he hypothesizes] that there were people here not long after the dispersal of humans from Africa 60,000 to 80,000 years ago."[9] This would suggest that the original inhabitants of the Americas were of a Negroid stock and not a Mongolian stock, the latter not entering the Americas until after the last ice age. So when the Mongolian stock arrived in the Americas it was already populated by Negroid people.

REVEALING AMERICA'S DARK SKINNED PAST

One must also assume that it is the mixing of these populations, at multiple and varying degrees, which created the numerous Negroid indigenous cultures of the Americas.

RED SILVERFOX THUNDERBIRD

The Mound Builders

WHEN THE EUROPEANS FIRST ARRIVED to what is now southeastern United States, they encountered a Negroid (often described as copper colored) culture of people that later became known as the Mound Builders. Mound Builders is a general term referring to the indigenous inhabitants of North America who constructed various styles of earthen mounds for burial, residential and ceremonial purposes.

The Mississippian Mound Builders dated from 1000 C.E.-1700 C.E. [C.E.- refers to the Christian or Common Era] is the culture that the Europeans encountered, and this culture is considered to be probably the most advanced society that arose in North America. This was a city-building society, supported by agriculture, and marked by

REVEALING AMERICA'S DARK SKINNED PAST

the building of pyramid-like mounds.10

Artist rendition of a mound city.

The cities consisted of enormous conical pyramids, excavated areas, vast terraces, irrigation canals, wells, ponds, underground passages and causeways, all of them constructed in a manner so substantial that they remain perfectly discernible until this day.11 According to competent engineers, it would take several thousands of our workmen, provided with all the resources of our grand modern industries, long years to erect some of their monuments, among which there are such as rival the Egyptian pyramids in grandeur... The number of these grand monuments is almost incalculable.12 The idea that American Indians could have built something resembling a city was so foreign to European settlers...they commonly thought they must have been the work of a foreign civilization: Phoenicians or Vikings or perhaps a lost Tribe of Isreal.13

The Mississippians were also great agriculturalists. They built vast canal systems that connected lakes that could be followed for hundreds of miles. These canals were created not only to irrigate the dry lands, but also provided the means for the society to flourish through trade with neighboring cultures.

The remnants of these cities, artifacts, mound structures which mimic celestial body movement and compare in size to the Egyptian pyramids, kiln burned pottery, etc. indicate that the indigenous cultures of America were not the savages that history has taught us they were. And, if we make another step into our study of their relics, we shall be compelled to admit that they were extraordinarily skillful, advanced in art, and not deprived of a high degree of science not expected to be found among so ancient a nation.14

REVEALING AMERICA'S DARK SKINNED PAST

RED SILVERFOX THUNDERBIRD

Types of Mounds

Conical Mound- Salem, NC

THERE WERE BASICALLY THREE TYPES of mounds that were constructed by the Mound Builders. The most common mounds are *Conical Mounds* which are mounds that are cone or oval shaped. Many of these types of mounds were for burial purposes, and the deceased was probably someone of importance in the society. Burial mounds ranged in height from three feet to twenty five feet. Conical mounds that weren't burial mounds can have a height up to seventy feet.

The *Earthen Lodge*, which is another type of Conical Mound, usually had a fire pit in the center and was used to hold important meetings amongst the chiefs.

The passageway into the Ocmulgee Earthen Lodge was built so that the rising sun shines inside twice a year (either on the spring/fall equinox or the summer/ winter solstice) onto the bird effigy platform, a raised platform where the three most important chiefs sat during those important meetings.

Ocmulgee Earthen Lodge Macon, GA

Passageway into Ocmulgee Earth Lodge

The second type of mounds is *Effigy Mounds* which are mounds that are built in the shape of animals, symbols, religious or human figures. It is believed that Effigy Mounds were utilized as sacred ceremonial grounds which enhanced communication with ancient ancestor spirits, along with augmenting the powers of healing.

REVEALING AMERICA'S DARK SKINNED PAST

Bird Effigy Platform

Serpent Mound, Adams County, Ohio 1330 ft.

Bear Mounds National Monument
Marquette, IA

The *Ten Marching Bears* at Effigy Mounds National Monument in Marquette, Iowa precisely shadows the Big Dipper in early spring as it marches around Polaris, the North Star.15

REVEALING AMERICA'S DARK SKINNED PAST

Artist interpretation of
sacred ceremony
surrounding Bear Mound

The last type of mounds are *Platform Mounds* or *Temple Mounds* which are flat topped mounds that were utilized to house temples for the leaders, sometimes for residences, sometimes for religious or ceremonial purposes, and sometimes for observing the waterways for unwanted visitors.

Platform Mound- Etowah Mound site, Cartersville, GA

MOUND SITES

WHAT IS PROBABLY THE OLDEST large scale mound site discovered in the United States is the Watson Brake Mounds, located in the floodplain of the Ouachita River in northern Louisiana near Monroe. This site consist of at least 11 mounds from three to 25 feet tall connected by ridges to form an oval 853 feet across, and it has been dated to the *Middle Archaic period, 3400 BCE, which would pre-date the erection of the pyramids in Egypt.

*(The indigenous cultures of the Americas have been divided into three eras: The Archaic Era-approximately 8,000 BCE [before the common or Christian Era] to 1,000 BCE, the Woodland Era-

approximately 1,000 BCE- 1,000 CE, and the Mississippian Era- approximately 1000 CE to 1700.)

Artist rendition of the Watson Brake

Some of the more recent archeological discoveries in the United States which deserve mention here (even though they aren't mounds) are the Shell Ring Complexes which are basically located along the shorelines of South Carolina, Georgia and Florida. The Sapelo Shell Ring Complex located on Sapelo Island off the coast of Georgia, is an ancient city [that] was constructed around 2300 B.C. and featured three neighborhoods each surrounded by circular walls twenty feet in height constructed from tons of seashells. Some of the earliest pottery in North America was also found buried in the remains of this lost city.16

Both Watson Brake and the Shell Ring Complexes pre-date the building of many of Egypt's pyramids.

Poverty Point

The oldest mound complex discovered in the United States is the Poverty Point Earthworks- in northeastern Louisiana in what is now Epps, LA. This complex is dated to the Late Archaic period- between the years 2000 BCE-1000 BCE.

The basic construction of the complex consists of six rows of ridges, which at one time were five feet high. Historians believe that these ridges served as foundations for dwellings for the inhabitants. The five aisles and six sections of ridges form a partial octagon, and the diameter of the outermost ridges measures three-quarters of a mile. The entire complex sits on more than 400 acres and has been estimated that approximately four to six thousand people may have lived there.

Bird Mound- Poverty

There are five earthen mounds located at Poverty Point. The largest mound, which is also the second largest mound found in present day United States, is a T-shaped mound called Bird Mound. This mound stands more than 70 feet high, measuring 640 feet along the wing and 710 feet from head to tail. That would make Bird Mound relatively the size of a professional baseball field. The mound got its name because it resembles a bird in flight.

Mound B, as it is called, is conical shaped- 180 feet in diameter and 20 feet in height, and the remaining three mounds at Poverty Point are platform mounds. In the center of the complex is the plaza; a flat, open area covering about 37 acres.

Artifacts found on the site show these people possessed great craftsmanship and were involved in long-distance trading networks. Here we find objects made of soapstone from Georgia and Alabama, lead ore from Missouri, copper from the Great Lakes, diverse stone tools from Alabama, Tennessee, Kentucky, Ohio, Indiana, Arkansas and Mississippi. Poverty Point societies loved exotic materials and crafted them into fine ornaments.[17]

REVEALING AMERICA'S DARK SKINNED PAST

Artist rendition of Cahokia Mound

The largest mound complex in present day United States is the Cahokia Mound complex found less than 10 miles outside of St. Louis in Cahokia, Illinois. The centerpiece of the complex is Monk's Mound, named for the French Monks who occupied the abandoned complex after their arrival here in North America. This colossal flat topped mound stands about 10 stories high, making it the tallest mound found in the United States. The mound covers over 14 acres, contains more than 22 million feet of soil, and it is larger at its base than the Great Pyramid of Khufu, the largest of the three pyramids of Giza in Egypt.

RED SILVERFOX THUNDERBIRD

Monk's Mound

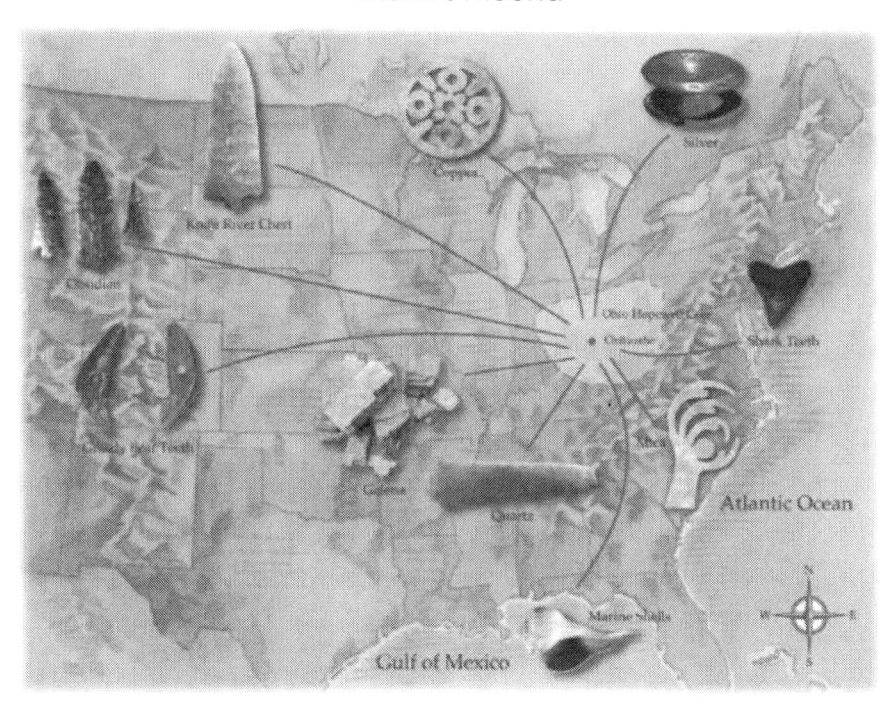

Cahokia Grand

The Cahokia complex was inhabited from the years 700 CE to approximately 1400. The culture reached its zenith around the 13th century. During its zenith, there were over 20,000 people living there, making it larger than London was at the same time. The city covered 6 square miles which would make the city comparable in size to Washington, D.C. The grand plaza, which was the size of about 45 football fields, was used for various activities such as sporting events and religious celebrations. There were enormous agricultural fields outside of the city which supplied the inhabitants their sustenance. The homes for the occupants were built in rows around various open plazas. Originally, there were over 120 mounds built there, while 80 remain there today.

The trading networks of Cahokia were vast. Importing copper from the Great Lakes, black chert from Oklahoma and Arkansas, mica from North Carolina, shells from the Gulf of Mexico, salt and lead from Illinois, and stone from Wyoming, Cahokia united a trading empire larger than the combined area of France, the United Kingdom, Spain, Germany, Austria, Italy, Belgium, the Netherlands, Ireland, Greece, Denmark, Romania, Switzerland, (former) Czechoslovakia, Portugal, Luxembourg, and Bulgaria.18 The bauxite stone used for Cahokia Woman (notice the Negroid features) comes from a tropical climate, and is a derivative of basalt, which is found in the Tuxtla Mountains in Mexico. Basalt volcanic rock is the material used for the infamous colossal Olmec heads.

REVEALING AMERICA'S DARK SKINNED PAST

Cahokia

THE OLMEC CIVILIZATION

ANOTHER NEGROID MOUND BUILDING CULTURE of North America which must be mentioned are the Olmec of Mexico. The Olmec are believed to be the first major culture in Mesoamerica and the mother culture of all the Mesoamerican civilizations that followed. The Olmec culture is recorded to have existed from approximately 1500 BCE to 400 BCE in the tropical lowlands of south-central Mexico. The Olmec built permanent complexes at San Lorenzo, Tres Zapotes, Laguna de los Cerros, and La Venta; each supplying their own natural resources valuable to the Olmec economy. Of those complexes, La Venta rose to be the grandest.

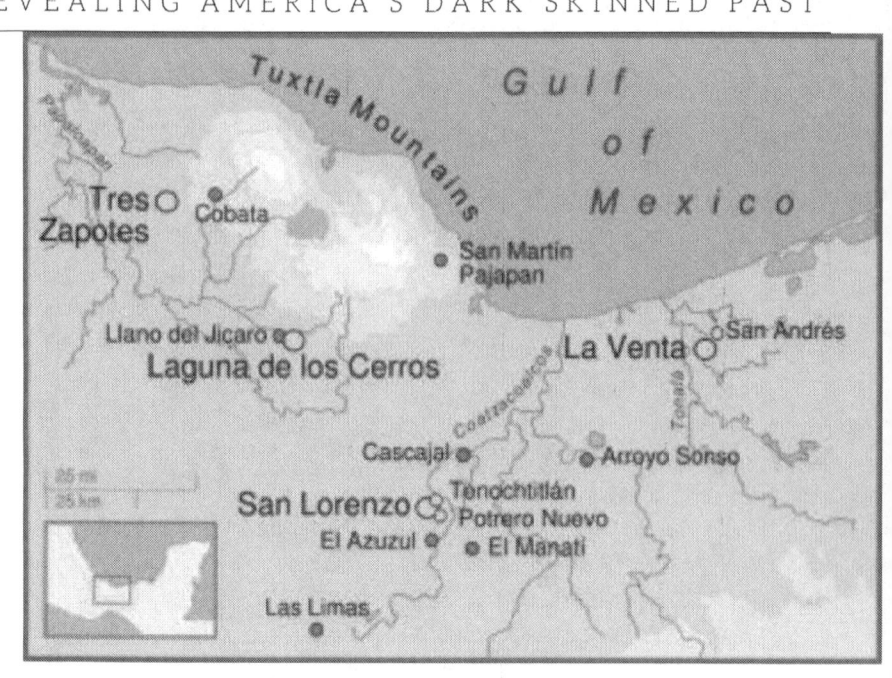

Olmec heartland

Olmec Throne

The La Venta complex is believed to have been in its grandeur from 1500 BCE to 1200 BCE. It consisted of several conical and platform mounds, along with have been the thrones for the rulers, and monuments-consisting of 3 colossal heads.

The centerpiece of La Venta is the Great Pyramid. This pyramidal mound stands today, over 3000 years after being built at 110 ft. high, with a diameter of 459 ft., and it covers an area of 2 square miles. It is the largest mound found in North America. The entire La Venta complex is built 8 degrees west of north, the same as pyramids of Giza in Egypt.

La Venta Great Pyramid

REVEALING AMERICA'S DARK SKINNED PAST

Aerial view of Pyramids of Giza

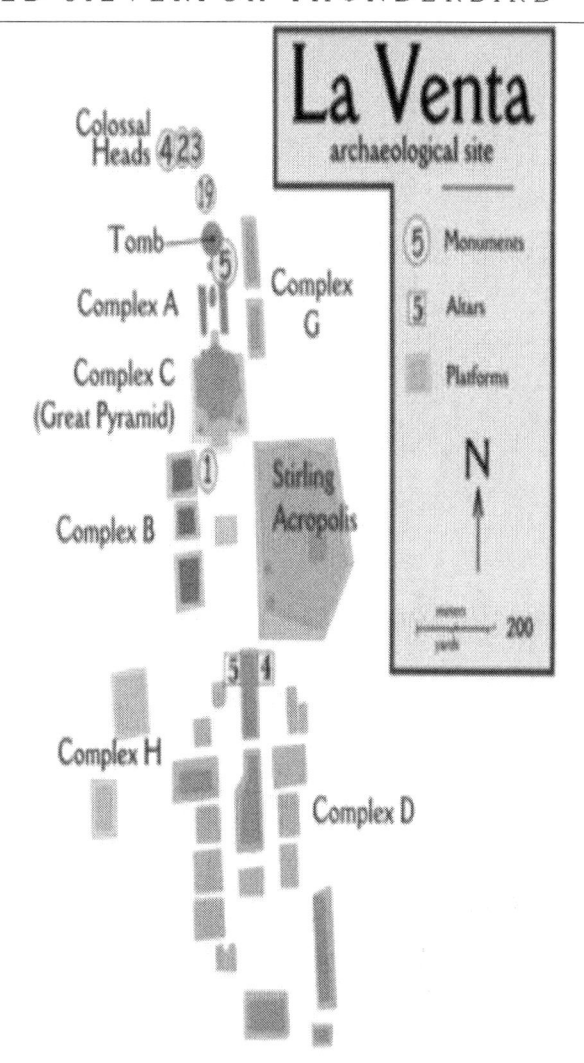

La Venta complex

REVEALING AMERICA'S DARK SKINNED PAST

The Olmec culture was first characterized as an art style through artifacts which collectors purchased in the late 19th century and early 20th century. The most recognizable Olmec artifacts, however, are the colossal heads which were first discovered in 1862. Seventeen of these heads have been discovered so far as they all were completely buried underground. Each head is unique, and carved out of one solid piece of volcanic basalt; the only source of this basalt is from the Tuxtla Mountains which are over 100 miles away from the La Venta complex. Because of their size, and their weight, some are up to nine feet tall and weigh between 25-55 tons; no one knows exactly how they were transported from the mountains to the complexes. Some people have surmised that moving a colossal head required the efforts of 1,500 people and taking approximately three to four months for it to arrive at its destination.

Excavated Olmec Head

Other Olmec artifacts which are considered to be very

sophisticated were made out of materials such as jade, obsidian, and magnetite which came from distances up to 250 miles away. This would suggest that the Olmec had a very extensive trading network. Olmec artwork includes sculptures and ceramics which were produced in kilns able of surpassing 900 degrees Celsius. The only other known culture that was able to achieve those high temperatures was Ancient Egypt, however there is growing evidence of ancient kilns in other American cultures.

The Olmec were also the first Mesoamerican culture to develop a writing system, a calendar, and the concept of zero.

Olmec ceramic

RED SILVERFOX THUNDERBIRD

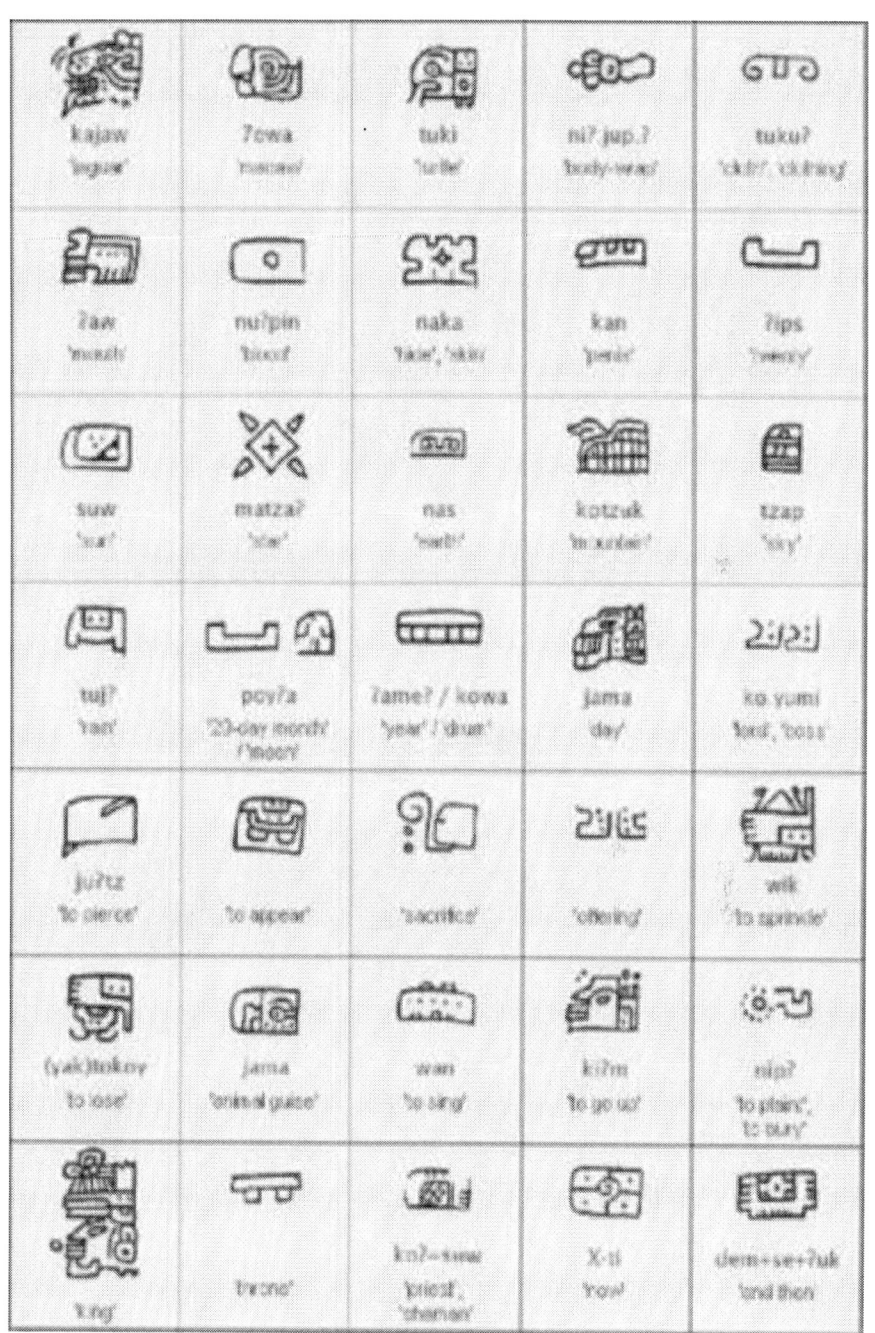

kajaw 'jaguar'	?owa 'macaw'	tuki 'turtle'	ni? jup.? 'body-wrap'	tuku? 'club?', 'clubing'
?aw 'mouth'	nu?pin 'blood'	naka 'hide', 'skin'	kan 'penis'	?ips 'weary'
suw 'sun'	matza? 'star'	nas 'earth'	kotzuk 'in xotoc?'	tzap 'sky'
tuj? 'rain'	poy?a '20-day month' / 'moon'	?ame? / kowa 'year' / 'blue'	jama 'day'	ko yumi 'lord', 'boss'
ju?tz 'to pierce'	'to appear'	'sacrifice'	'offering'	wik 'to sprinkle'
(yak)tokoy 'to lose'	jama 'animal guise'	wan 'to sing'	ki?m 'to go up'	nip? 'to plant', 'to bury'
'king'	'throne'	ko?-xwe 'priest', 'shaman'	X-ti 'now'	dem+se+?uk 'and then'

Example of Olmec Hieroglyphs

REVEALING AMERICA'S DARK SKINNED PAST

Examples of the Colossal Olmec Heads

As you can see, the Colossal Olmec Heads along with other (but not all) Olmec artifacts contain prominent Negroid features. Many historians want to dismiss that the Olmec were of a Negroid stock. Nonetheless, the study of art forms is a reliable indicator of the racial type of the communities in which the art works were created.[19]

There have been connections that suggest a relationship between the Olmec and the other

Mesoamerican cultures to the Mound building cultures of the United States, especially of the Mississippians or what they are sometimes referred to, the Southern Cult of Southeastern United States.

Carvings in stone, metal tools and ceremonial artifacts, fragments of textiles and works of art share imagery with Mesoamerican sources. The pottery at Ocmulgee National Monument in central Georgia is virtually identical to the Maya Plain Red pottery made by Maya Commoners.[20]

Olmec Art

REVEALING AMERICA'S DARK SKINNED PAST

Mayan Art

Mississippian Art

Another similarity is the agriculture. Corn and beans, whose origins are in Mexico, was a defining characteristic of the Mississippian tribes. Most agronomists [are] convinced that corn, beans, and tobacco came to the natives of the United States and Canada from Mexico.[21]

One of the most striking similarities is the construction of the ancient cities of North America. There is a strong similarity in the architectural forms and town plans between southern Mexico and the Southeastern United States.[22]

Clearly something was going on: embossed copper, engraved marine shell, stone figures,...are all representative of this pan-continental movement.[23]

REVEALING AMERICA'S DARK SKINNED PAST

THE DESTRUCTION OF ANCIENT CITIES AND ARTIFACTS

FROM THE MOMENT OF THE ARRIVAL of the European to the North American continent, many of the indigenous cultures began to show signs of decline. The lack of historical information led some to believe that these societies were the victims of some sort of extinction. But new archaeological evidence shows that the process was one of replacement and social evolution.[24]

The burden of the lack of historical information lay directly in the hands of the conquering Europeans, and later to the European settlers. As stated previously, when the Europeans arrived to the shores of North America they encountered Negroid societies, and the conquerors did not want to leave evidence behind of advanced Negroid cultures that exhibited systems of civilization.

Many of the descriptions of the indigenous people of the Americas describe people of a dark complexion. There were people in Panama that were described as such: "These people are identical with the Negroes we have seen in Guinea [Africa]."25

In the early 1560's a Spanish official wrote to the king that in the island of Puerto Rico there are above 15,000 negroes and less than 500 Spaniards and in all of Hispaniola there may be 2,000 Spaniards and there are over 30,000 negroes... The same is the case in the island of Cuba and in Vera Cruz, Puerto de Cavallos, which is in Honduras, and in Nombre de Dios, Carthagena, Santa Maria and the coast of Venezuela, where there are twenty negroes to one white man.26

Negro was a terminology that defined a person of a dark complexion. The term Negro or its equivalent was not used for race [a concept that in the early 1500's had not yet developed] or for a single stock of people or to point to ancestry or ethnicity. It was usually a single description for perceived color or appearance.27 And Negro was one of many terminologies that was used to define the indigenous inhabitants of the North America.

So when Christopher Columbus and the other explorers and conquerors began to navigate the Americas, they immediately began to utilize the indigenous people and began their destruction of the indigenous cultures. Of course, slavery was a major factor in the destruction of numerous indigenous tribes and nations in North America, but another just as disparaging factor was the destruction of the ancient cities and artifacts that would completely conceal the true identities of the original inhabitants of this continent. Remember, the Europeans needed to remove everything that would not benefit their existence in the 'New World', and it was imperative to remove any remnants of 'civilized' living.

One of the most glaring examples of this destruction was the virtual total obliteration of Mayan artifacts. After the Spanish conquest of the Yucatan, Diego de Landa Calderon, a Franciscan friar, was sent there in 1549 to Christianize the indigenous Maya people. By 1552, he was in charge of the convent of the important town of Izamal; and by 1561, he held the highest position available at the time in the religious hierarchy of Yucatan, as the provincial or head of the Franciscan province.[28]

The next year after this appointment, he ordered an Inquisition against the native inhabitants of the area, accusing them of idolatry. He destroyed almost all of the original Mayan writings claiming they were tainted by superstitions. Many of these writings were sacred writings and the history of the Mayan people and their culture.

Landa was shown these works in confidence because the Mayan people believed he was a man of honor.

Along with the destruction of the writings, he also destroyed thousands of artifacts and thousands of sculptures and works of art, declaring that they were works of pagans. He was accused by his own associates of excessive cruelty against the people and was sent back to Spain to address these charges. While in Spain, perhaps feeling remorseful of his destructive deeds, he wrote a book about the Mayan entitled *Yucatan Before and After the Conquest*. Ninety nine percent of what we know of the Mayas, we know as a result either of what Landa has told us...or have learned in the use and study of what he told [in his book].[29] So what we today know of Mayan history is from what Diego de Landa wrote in his book.

So, if ninety-nine hundredths of our knowledge is at base derived from what he told us, it is an equally safe statement that at that Auto de fe [Inquisition] of '62, he burned ninety-nine times as much knowledge of Maya history and sciences as he has given us in his book.[30] No one will ever know the history that was lost in the volumes of history of the Maya that was destroyed, nor will we know how much of the information that Landa wrote is tainted with European bias.

Page from Yucatan Before and After the Conquest
showing Mayan hieroglyphs

REVEALING AMERICA'S DARK SKINNED PAST

RED SILVERFOX THUNDERBIRD

"TO THE WAYS OF THE WHITE PEOPLE"

QUOTE BY THOMAS JEFFERSON

Before · After Indian Boarding school

THE DESTRUCTION OF THE INDIGENOUS CULTURES became the hallmark of exploration and colonization in the Americas. The indigenous people along with their artifacts and enormous complexes were in the way of colonial progress, and removing these things became a prerequisite to the success of the colonies.

The first step to accomplish this with the Spanish was through the mission system. Spanish missions were explicitly established for the purpose of religious conversion and instruction in the Catholic faith. However, the mission system actually served as the primary means of integrating Indians into the political and economic structure of Florida's colonial system.[31] It was believed that by replacing the spiritual practices of the indigenous people with Christianity, not only would it save their souls, it would be easier to assimilate those populations into colonial living, and, to quote Thomas Jefferson, "to the ways of the white people". Missionaries and officials agreed that as Indians became Christians they would naturally adopt lifeways that would make them Americans, and vice versa.

Once the native populations were converted to Christianity and accepted European ideologies, and all signs of 'Indianess' were removed, it was believed the native cultures would become totally assimilated into white society, the native people would become extinct and "they would live happy lives forever under the protective benevolence of the United States".[33] Spanish efforts to eliminate Indian religious practices resulted in the rampant destruction of anything Indian.[34]

This application of destroying anything Indian is a practice that began as early as the first European contact and unbelievably, is still happening even into the 21st century. What initially began as a conversion of religious practices, then converted into the destruction of artifacts and the culture, then transformed into an apparent extermination of the Indian nations. While the latter was not totally effective, what is still being accomplished is the eradication of some of what was once the most visible artifacts, namely the Native American mounds.

Once the United States government was successful in pushing the indigenous inhabitants further and further inland, eventually beyond the Mississippi River into 'Indian Country' and totally away from their ancestral lands, it was not long before the ancient Native American villages and mounds started being demolished.

From the eighteenth century until nearly through the twentieth, archaeology handled the mounds quite poorly, leading to two centuries' worth of the "slaughter" of...mounds. Until the 1940's, archaeologist and hobbyists (it was sometimes hard to tell the difference) ripped the mounds open for little more than idle curiosity's sake.[35]

After the Creek War in 1836, removal of the Creek Native American inhabitants began in Georgia ejecting them from the Ocmulgee Mound village and from Native American ancestral land which covered much of Georgia. By early 1837, over 14,000 Creeks had been removed to Oklahoma. By 1840, large oak trees were being cut down off the mounds for timber, and much of the mound site was turned into a plantation. By 1843, a railroad was being cut through the mound site, destroying part of the Lesser Temple Mound. In 1874 a second huge cut for a railroad (still in use) is [was] excavated through the mound area and destroys[ed] a large portion of the Funeral Mound. According to Charles C. Jones, in his book, Antiquities of the Southern Indians, many relics and human burials were removed during this work.[36]

In 1876, it was a Sabbath pastime to open "Indian mounds" in the forenoon and in the afternoon to shoot the skulls thus obtained full of holes as a test of marksmanship.[37] Hundreds of burial mounds located in the great central valleys were ruthlessly ransacked and left partly destroyed by scholars and vandals alike.[38]

REVEALING AMERICA'S DARK SKINNED PAST

Big Mound Late 1800's

Big Mound today

Big Mound at Cahokia, what was once one of the largest burial mounds in the United States standing at 30 feet high and 300 feet long took years to dismantle. Local residents, like most United States citizens, considered Native American mounds as convenient sources of dirt, most dirt being utilized as fill dirt for roads or for railroad beds.

There was formerly a large five-sided mound on the Oconaluftee River in the Birdtown section of the North Carolina Cherokee Reservation. Its town site was gradually destroyed by development in the middle to late 20th century.[37]

In Philadelphia, PA a very large temple mound was utilized as a reservoir to supply water to the residents of the city. Today, the Philadelphia Museum of Art sits atop this massive mound.

Fair Mount
Philadelphia, PA- Mid 1800's

Fairmount Water
Works-Late 1800's

Philadelphia
Museum of Art

Most Native American mounds in the United States today are barely noticeable. Many are covered over from decades upon decades of neglect while others have been utilized as fixtures on American golf courses.

Myrtle Beach Golf Course, South Carolina

EPILOGUE

EVEN WHILE NEW INFORMATION is being revealed in science about how and when the Americas got populated, academia is still reluctant to disseminate this information. Why does academia continue to promote the Bering Strait theory as to how the Americas got populated, when there are more and more discoveries that disprove this theory? Is it that it will be revealed that the original inhabitants of the Americas were actually a Negroid stock and not a Mongolian stock, and when the Mongolians finally migrated, they mixed in with the Negroid stock that was already here? Is it that it will expose how history has not been candid about the existence of Blacks in the Americas and has omitted this information to the benefit of Eurocentric rationale? Or is it that volumes upon volumes of books must be rewritten and the mindset of historians and society in general must be completely reoriented?

Whatever the reason, it is time for this information to

stop being suppressed and making it inaccessible to the majority of populations around the world. It is time to remove the chains of oppression that have been on our collective minds for centuries. The time is now for this American Deception to be unveiled.

REVEALING AMERICA'S DARK SKINNED PAST

RED SILVERFOX THUNDERBIRD

About the Author

RENEE SANDERS IS THE CO-FOUNDER of InDEED-Indigenous Education Enrichment and Development, an indigenous non-profit organization which focuses on educating people of the forgotten and omitted history of people of color in what is now the United States. She received her formal education at Temple University in Philadelphia, PA where she received her Bachelor's degree in Music Education. She also received her Middle Years certification and Reading Endorsement from the Atlanta Public Schools in Atlanta, GA.

Educating people has been a lifetime passion of Renee, having spent over 30 years as a teacher in Philadelphia and Atlanta where she has taught: general music classes; band classes; instrumental music lessons; reading classes; language arts tutoring classes; and health classes. She has also worked as a long term elementary substitute teacher and was also the principal of a private day school. Prior to starting her teaching career, Renee spent several years working with children as a music coach and as a summer camp counselor.

Drawing on decades of her music teaching experience where she focused on exposing her students to the evolution of music in America, Renee now focuses on educating people of the under exposed history of people of color in the United States before and after the arrival of the Europeans. She, along with her son and co-founder of InDEED Tavis Sanders, have created educational videos that air not only in Philadelphia and New York on cable television but have also been viewed in over 195 countries on their YouTube channel.

Renee is very optimistic that by bringing to light this previously neglected and overlooked information, that people will have a better picture of the past to use to make sense of the present and have the ability to create a better future for all.

http://indedu.org/reneebio

RED SILVERFOX THUNDERBIRD

Bibliography

1. www.grazian-archive.com
2. The First Americans were Africans- p. 32
3. Ibid p. 35
4. www.nytimes.com/2011/03/25/science/25archeo.html?pagewanted=all
5. The Cycle of Cosmic Catastrophes: By Richard Firestone, Allen West, Simon Warwick-Smith p. 81
6. www.sciencedaily.com/releases/2004/11/041118104010.htm
7. http://news.nationalgeographic.com/news/2008/09/080903-oldest-skeletons.html
8. www.sciencedaily.com/releases/2004/11/041118104010.htm
9. www.allendale-expedition.net/pressreleases/AJC18earlyman.pdf
10. The Mound Builders of Ancient North America E. Barrie Kavasch p.29
11. History of America before Columbus- Peter DeRoo p. 61
12. Ibid p.73-74
13. http://ngm.nationalgeographic.com/2011/01/cahokia/hodges-text/2
14. History of America before Columbus p. 67
15. The Mound Builders of Ancient North America E. Barrie Kavasch p.29
16. http://lostworlds.org/ancient-walled-city-older-egypts-pyramids-unearthed-georgia-coast/
17. The Mound Builders of Ancient North America E. Barrie Kavasch p. 12

18. Modern Tribal Development- Dean Howard Smith p. 25
19. www.white-history.com
20. www.examiner.com/article/ruins-georgia-mountains-show-evidence-of-maya-connection
21. Ibid
22. Ibid
23. www.digitalhistory.uh.edu/database/article_display.cfm?HHID=660
24. Modern Tribal Development- Dean Howard Smith p. 26
25. Early America Revisited By Ivan Van Sertima p.30
26. Africans and Native Americans p. 78
27. Ibid p. 66
28. The Decipherment of Ancient Maya Writing- by Stephen D. Houston, Oswaldo Fernando Chinchilla Mazariegos, David Stuart p. 29
29. Yucatan Before and After the Conquest- by Diego de Landa Calderone-translation Wm. Gates p. 2
30. Ibid p. 3
31. www.georgiaencyclopedia.org/nge/Article.jsp?id=h-572
32. The Last Indian War- by Elliot West p. 54
33. http://digital.library.okstate.edu/Oakerhater/essay.html
34. The History of Mexico- by Burton Kirkwood p. 54
35. www.nps.gov/ocmu/historyculture/index.htm
36. Records of the Past- Records of the Past Exploration Society- G. Frederick Wright, Frederick B. Wright p.335
37. www.examiner.com/article/native-americans-buit-chain-of-five-sided-mounds-across-southeast

Made in the USA
San Bernardino, CA
10 August 2020